THE GRACE OF REPENTANCE

The

GRACE

of

REPENTANCE

SINCLAIR FERGUSON

WHEATON, ILLINOIS

Published by Crossway
        1300 Crescent Street
        Wheaton, Illinois 60187

The Alliance of Confessing Evangelicals exists to call the church, amidst our dying culture, to repent of its worldliness, to recover and confess the truth of God's Word as did the Reformers, and to see that truth embodied in doctrine, worship, and life.

Cover design: Studio Gearbox

Cover photo: iStock

First printing 2000

Reprinted with new cover 2011

Printed in the United States of America

ISBN 13: 978-1-4335-1983-3
ISBN 10: 1-4335-1983-6
ePub ISBN: 978-1-4335-1986-4
Mobipocket ISBN: 978-1-4335-1985-7
PDF ISBN: 978-1-4335-1984-0

Library of Congress Cataloging-in-Publication Data

Ferguson, Sinclair B.
   The grace of repentance / Sinclair B. Ferguson.
   p.   cm. — (Today's issues)
   Includes bibliographical references.
   ISBN 1-58134-165-2 (trade pbk. : alk. paper)
   1. Repentance—Biblical teaching. I. Title. II. Today's issues
(Wheaton, Ill.)
BS680.R36 F47   2000
234'.5—dc21   99-045156

Crossway is a publishing ministry of Good News Publishers.

VP		19	18	17	16	15	14	13	12	11
15	14	13	12	11	10	9	8	7	6	5	4	3	2	1

CONTENTS

PREFACE

These are not good days for the evangelical church, and anyone who steps back from what is going on for a moment to try to evaluate our life and times will understand that.

In the last few years a number of important books have been published all trying to understand what is happening, and they are saying much the same thing even though the authors come from fairly different backgrounds and are doing different work. One is by David F. Wells, a theology professor at Gordon-Conwell Theological Seminary in Massachusetts. It is called *No Place for Truth*. A second is by Michael Scott Horton, vice president of the Alliance of Confessing Evangelicals. His book is called *Power Religion*. The third is by the well-known pastor of Grace Community Church in California, John F. MacArthur. It is called *Ashamed of the Gospel*. Each of these authors is writing about the evangelical church, not the liberal church, and a person can get an idea of what each is saying from the titles alone.

Yet the subtitles are even more revealing. The subtitle

of Wells's book reads *Or Whatever Happened to Evangelical Theology?* The subtitle of Horton's book is *The Selling Out of the Evangelical Church*. The subtitle of John MacArthur's work proclaims, *When the Church Becomes Like the World*.

When you put these together, you realize that these careful observers of the current church scene perceive that today evangelicalism is seriously off base because it has abandoned its evangelical truth-heritage. The thesis of David Wells's book is that the evangelical church is either dead or dying as a significant religious force because it has forgotten what it stands for. Instead of trying to do God's work in God's way, it is trying to build a prosperous earthly kingdom with secular tools. Thus, in spite of our apparent success we have been "living in a fool's paradise," Wells declared in an address to the National Association of Evangelicals in 1995.

John H. Armstrong, a founding member of the Alliance of Confessing Evangelicals, has edited a volume titled *The Coming Evangelical Crisis*. When he was asked not long afterwards whether he thought the crisis was still coming or is actually here, he admitted that in his judgment the crisis is already upon us.

The Alliance of Confessing Evangelicals is addressing this problem through seminars and conferences, radio programs, *modern* REFORMATION magazine, Reformation Societies, and scholarly writings. The series of booklets on today's issues is a further effort along these same lines. If you are troubled by the state of today's church and are helped by these booklets, we invite you to contact the Alliance at 1716 Spruce Street, Philadelphia, PA 19103. You can also phone us at 215-546-3696 or visit the Alliance at our website: www. AllianceNet.org. We would like to work with you under God "for a modern Reformation."

James Montgomery Boice
Alliance of Confessing Evangelicals

CHAPTER ONE

THE MONK'S TALE

t was the year 1517. Europe was a Roman Catholic continent, and Leo X was Pope, a man "as elegant and as indolent as a Persian cat," as Roland Bainton described him (*Here I Stand* [Nashville: Abingdon, 1978], p. 56). Leo needed money to complete a great building project already underway, a new St. Peter's being built to replace its condemned predecessor. Leo needed lots of money! Huge, superabundant resources of money!

The intrigue that unfolded reads like a modern novel. Albert of Brandenburg wanted the archbishopric of Mainz and the primacy of all Germany that would come with it. So he borrowed money from the great German banking house of Fugger, paid the Pope, and in exchange was granted not only the archbishopric but the privilege of granting indulgences in his territory for eight years. Indulgences could release souls from the pains of purgatory for extended periods of time, perhaps forever. The deal was complex, however. Albert needed to clear his loan. But in addition, any further "profits" would be split 50/50 between St. Peter's and Fugger's Bank.

The new primate needed an ecclesiastical salesman to raise the money, and such a man was available in the great indulgence vendor Johannes Tetzel. Tetzel had mastered the art of communicating to sons and daughters the pleas of their dead parents to deliver them from the flames in which they languished. When he was promoted for his Doctor's degree Tetzel had defended the thesis:

> *As soon as the coin in the coffer springs*
> *The soul from purgatory springs.*

That had been the teaching of Pope Sixtus IV, it was Tetzel's gospel, and by and large that was then the condition of Christianity.

In the fall of 1517, the great indulgence-monger was near enough to the parish of Wittenberg for parishioners to flock out to hear him and buy his wares. At the end of the month, on the eve of All Saints Day, a troubled and distressed thirty-three-year-old monk of the Augustinian order made his way quietly to the Castle Church and posted on the door a placard listing a series of theological points he was prepared to debate and defend. He was not a well-known or popular figure. He was a professor of Bible, a scholar, and a teacher. His theses were written in Latin, which the common people did not understand. He had no idea that his action would produce a spiritual revolution.

The monk's name was Martin Luther, and his placard was the now famous Ninety-Five Theses, a document that has probably been more influential in history than either the British Magna Charta or the American Declaration of Independence.

Luther's theses contained statements of church-shattering importance and led to what we call the Protestant Reformation. They are widely hailed as one of the great evangelical statements in history. Every year they are celebrated at Reformation Day Services. Still today Christians defend tough positions by an appeal to Luther's principle, "Here I stand, I can do no other. God help me."

The first of Luther's theses put the axe to the root of the tree of medieval theology:

> When our Lord and Master, Jesus Christ, said "repent," he meant that the entire life of believers should be one of repentance.

Luther had been studying the new edition of the Greek New Testament published by the humanist scholar Erasmus. In these studies he had come to realize that the Latin Vulgate, the official church Bible, had misleadingly rendered "repent" in Matthew 4:17 by *poenitentiam agite* ("do penance"), thus completely misconstruing Jesus' meaning. Luther saw that the Gospel called not for an act of penance but for a radical change of mind that would lead to a deep transformation of life. Later he would write to his vicar Johannes Staupitz about this glowing discovery: "I venture to say they are wrong who make more of the act in Latin than of the change of heart in Greek" (Bainton, *Here I Stand,* p. 67).

So began the Reformation, and at its heart lay Luther's great discovery: Repentance is a characteristic of the whole life, not the action of a single moment. Salvation is a gift, received only in Christ, only by grace, only in faith. *But it is salvation,* and salvation means we are actually being saved. Otherwise we cannot have come to know Christ the Savior.

Is that how we think about repentance? Or do we tend to think of it as something we are glad to have behind us, never to be repeated? In today's church we are as likely to be told not only that we can become Christians without such repentance, but can even remain Christians without it, being *carnal* to the end of our days. By contrast, our forefathers were convinced that repentance is so central to the Gospel that without it there can be no salvation. They believed this because it is the Bible's teaching.

CHAPTER TWO

BIBLICAL
REPENTANCE

Since repentance is such an important concept for understanding the true biblical Gospel, it is not surprising to discover that the Scriptures have an extensive and lively vocabulary to describe it.

THE OLD TESTAMENT VOCABULARY

Two Old Testament metaphors express the rigor, thoroughness, and even pain that can be involved in repentance: circumcising one's heart (Jer. 4:4) and breaking up fallow ground with a plow (Hosea 10:12). *Shub*, the Hebrew word that dominates the language of repentance, is one of the most frequently used verbs in the Old Testament. It is used over 100 times in the book of Jeremiah alone. It means to change a course of action, to turn away, or to turn back. This turning can refer to apostasy, a turning *away* from God (Num. 14:43; Josh. 22:16, 18, 23, 29; 1 Sam. 15:11; 1 Kings 9:6); but predominantly it denotes man's turning away from rebellion against God, and turning *to* God. It means a complete about-turn.

This language occurs frequently within the context of God's covenant relations with his people. In that covenant God has made provision to be gracious to those who rebel against him. He therefore urges them to return to him, to plow up hearts that have become hardened, and to circumcise hearts that have been covered with the spirit of the world and the flesh.

The same verb is used in the Old Testament for the return of God's people from exile. Because of their rebellion, the people have been in the far country. But God has been gracious; now they must make the journey back to the place where he has promised to bless them. Repentance is the moral and spiritual equivalent of that geographical return. It is made possible only because of God's covenant mercy.

What is involved in such repentance? Two things:

1. *Recognizing that offenses have been committed against God and the covenant he has made with his people.* Psalm 51, where David recognizes that his sin is *against God only* (v. 4), reflects this covenant orientation. Likewise, Isaiah pictures

the people as covenant sons who have rebelled against their Father. The inevitable consequence is that they end up in the "far country" of exile, long since threatened in the Mosaic covenant (Deut. 28:36). Thus repentance involves recognition that we are under the covenant judgment of God for our rejection of the obligations of faith and obedience that we have to him (Deut. 28:15). It is the realization that the return journey involves reversing the outward and downward journey.

2. *Turning away from sin in view of the gracious provisions that the Lord has made for us in his covenant.* Repentance means returning to a spirit of creatureliness before the Creator in recognition of his mercy to penitent believers (Deut. 30:11-20). Ungodliness is thus rejected and righteousness is embraced. In the Old Testament this spirit of repentance is created by a sense of who God is and by an awareness of the true character of sin. It is a God-centered response, indeed the beginning of true God-centeredness. Turning away from sin and turning back to God belong together.

THE NEW TESTAMENT VOCABULARY

In the New Testament three verbs are used in connection with repentance. The first verb (*epistrepho*) emphasizes the idea of turning back and is used on a number of occasions for converting or returning to the Lord (Acts 26:20). The Thessalonians turned *to* God, *from* idols, to serve the living and true God (1 Thess. 1:9).

The second verb (*metamelomai*) occurs relatively rarely in the New Testament (Matt. 21:29, 32; 27:3; 2 Cor. 7:8; Heb. 7:21). It conveys the idea of regret. It is a state of mind that may or may not be accompanied by returning to God.

The third verb (*metanoeo*) is the New Testament's chief expression for repentance. In classical Greek it can mean to know or to become aware of something afterwards. This puts our past actions in a different light. Basically, *metanoeo* involves a change of mind. However, in the New Testament this carries significant implications. Repentance means a change of mind that leads to a change of lifestyle.

Ulrich Becker summarizes the New Testament teaching in these words:

> Repentance, penitence and conversion are closely linked. Whenever someone gives his thought and life a new direction, it always involves a judgment on his previous views and behavior. This is expressed in the NT by three word-groups which deal with its various aspects: *epistrepho*, *metamelomai* and *metanoeo*. The first and third both mean turn round, turn oneself round and refer to a man's conversion. This presupposes and includes a complete change under the influence of the Holy Spirit. *Metamelomai* expresses rather the feeling of repentance

for error, debt, failure and sin, and so it looks back. Hence it does not necessarily cause a man to turn to God. *Epistrepho* is probably the widest conception, because it always includes faith. (*New International Dictionary of New Testament Theology*, ed. Colin Brown [Grand Rapids, Mich.: Zondervan, 1975-78], vol. 1, pp. 353-354)

At first sight it might seem as if New Testament repentance no longer carries the covenantal overtones of the Old. But the reverse is the case. In the New Testament the covenant reaches its fulfillment in the coming of the Kingdom of God in Jesus Christ and the inauguration of the last days. The covenant promise is no longer foremost because it has been fulfilled. In a sense the covenant *is* Christ. The focus of attention is now no longer on a promise but on a person.

Hence, the message of the New Testament is not, "This is God's covenant; therefore repent." Instead it is, "The Kingdom of God has come in the person of Jesus; repent and believe in him." Kingdom-oriented and Christ-centered language now predominates, not because the covenant has been abandoned but because this has always been the focus of the covenant. The King has come. Therefore, to speak of his Kingdom and the necessity of repentance is to speak in the language of God's covenant grace!

It is precisely this Old Testament idea that Jesus turns

into a parable of God's grace in conversion in the story of the son who showed such prodigal indifference to his father and ended up in the "far country." Only later did the memory of the supplies in his father's house bring him to himself and then home to his father (Luke 15:11–32). The self-absorption of the son, his seeking pleasure rather than fellowship with his father, led to his bankruptcy in the far country. Only when he was awakened to his folly and, simultaneously, to the adequate provisions that even the servants in his father's house enjoyed did he begin the painful trek home. Like the exiles, the way back for the prodigal was by reversing the direction of his journey.

Biblical repentance, then, is not merely a sense of regret that leaves us where it found us. It is a radical reversal that takes us back along the road of our sinful wanderings, creating in us a completely different mind-set. We come to our senses spiritually (Luke 15:17). Thus the prodigal son's life was no longer characterized by the demand "give me" (v. 12) but now by the request "make me . . ." (v. 19).

This lies on the surface of the New Testament's teaching. Regret there will be, but the heart of repentance is the lifelong moral and spiritual turnaround of our lives as we submit to the Lord.

THE NECESSITY OF REPENTANCE

Repentance is essential for salvation. Twice in the same context Jesus underscores this: "Unless you repent, you too will all perish" (Luke 13:3, 5). God commands all men everywhere to repent, because he has fixed the day in which he will judge the world in righteousness by Christ (Acts 17:30-31). Repentance "is of such necessity to all sinners that none may expect pardon without it" (*Westminster Confession of Faith*, XV, 3).

Salvation is salvation from sin. That means more than forgiveness; it includes sanctification, a transformed life. It involves those who are saved in a turning away from sin. That turning away is repentance. There can be no salvation if we continue in sin (Rom. 6:1-4; 1 John 3:9).

Does this mean that we are forgiven on the basis of our repentance? Not at all! Repentance and faith are both necessary for salvation, but they are related to justification in different ways. Faith alone is the instrument by which Christ is received and rested on as Savior. Justification is by faith, not by repentance. But faith (and therefore justification) cannot exist where there is no repentance. Repentance is as necessary to salvation by faith as the ankle is to walking. The one does not act apart from the other. I cannot come to Christ in faith without turning from sin in repentance.

THE GRACE OF REPENTANCE

Faith is trusting in Christ; repentance is turning from sin. They are two sides of the same coin of belonging to Jesus.

ELEMENTS OF REPENTANCE

Repentance is not an abstract idea, however. It is the unique activity of various individuals. Therefore, it follows that the actual experience of repentance will vary from person to person, as will their consciousness of *their own* sin. God's mercy is not merely a universally applicable medicine for sin; it is prescribed for each individual's sinfulness, his or her particular guilt. The individual experience of repentance is bound to take a unique shape, though it also shares in a common pattern.

The great Dutch theologian Herman Bavinck wrote some wise words in this connection:

> Repentance is, despite its oneness in essence, different in form according to the persons in whom it takes place and the circumstances in which it takes place. The way upon which the children of God walk is one way but they are varyingly led upon that way, and have varying experiences. What a difference there is in the leading which God gives the several patriarchs; what a difference there is in the conversion of Manasseh, Paul and Timothy! How unlike are the experiences of a David and a Solomon, a John and a James! And that same difference we encounter

also outside of Scripture in the life of the church fathers, of the reformers, and of all the saints. The moment we have eyes to see the richness of the spiritual life, we do away with the practice of judging others according to our puny measure.

There are people who know of only one method, and who regard no one as having repented unless he can speak of the same spiritual experiences which they have had or claim to have had. But Scripture is much richer and broader than the narrowness of such confines. In this respect also the word applies: There are diversities of gifts but the same Spirit; and there are differences of administrations but the same Lord. And there are diversities of operations, but it is the same God which worketh all in all (1 Cor. 12:4-6).

The true repentance does not consist of what men make of it, but of what God says of it. In the diversity of providences and experiences it consists and must consist of the dying of the old and the rising of the new man. (*Our Reasonable Faith* [Grand Rapids, Mich.: Eerdmans, 1956], p. 438)

Within this general framework, there are several elements that are common to all incidences of biblical repentance.

1. *A new attitude toward sin.* This will inevitably be accompanied by a sense of shame and sorrow for our sin (Luke 15:18-19; Rom. 6:21). Two things should be noted:

First, repentance cannot be defined exclusively as shame and sorrow. Judas, for example, "repented" (Matt. 27:3, KJV), but this was not evangelical repentance. Rather, it was a sorrow that fed on itself and eventually led to despair and self-inflicted death. Paul called it a "worldly sorrow [that] brings death" (2 Cor. 7:10). By contrast, David's repentance, which was also marked by remorse and regret, was evangelical because it was God-centered, not self-centered. David recognized and responded to the fact that he had acted wickedly and committed sin *against God*. His repentance included the hope of forgiveness and new life (Ps. 51).

Second, this new attitude to sin will be as concrete as the sin to which the new attitude is directed. Since repentance means returning in a spirit of obedience back along the former path of disobedience, it is worked out in obedience to the specific commandments of God (Deut. 30:2). Thus, in the Gospels the repentance to which the rich young ruler was summoned was to develop self-denial in the very area that had been marked by self-indulgence— selling everything he possessed, giving his money to the poor, and then following Jesus. In the case of Zacchaeus, repentance meant returning what had been taken unjustly. Paul describes the repentance that issues from the regenerate heart as the righteous requirements of the Law being met in those who walk not according to the flesh but according to the Spirit (Rom. 8:4).

2. *A new attitude toward self.* Repentance also inevitably

involves a changed attitude toward myself. It means dying to the old ways, crucifying the flesh. Initial repentance is simply the beginning of an ongoing process in which the lifestyle of the old self is dismantled and put to death. Older writers used to call it "the mortification of sin."

Such repentance is *radical*. It involves agreeing with God's judgment on my sinful life, justifying God in his righteousness, and condemning myself in my sinfulness. It is taking up the cross, denying myself, putting off the old man (Eph. 4:22; Col. 3:9), and crucifying the flesh with its lusts (Gal. 5:24).

It is also *perpetual*. It means not even thinking about "how to gratify the desires of the sinful nature" (Rom. 13:14). Not ever! It was to Christians that Paul wrote these words, describing what a life of repentance means. It means ongoing, dogged, persistent refusal to compromise with sin. The Christian is a new person in Christ, but he is imperfectly renewed. He has died to sin and has been raised to new life. But this mortification and vivification continue throughout the whole course of his life on earth. We are no longer what we once were, but we are not yet what God calls us to become; and as long as that is the case we are called to an ongoing battle for holiness.

3. *A new attitude toward God.* Repentance also implies a changed attitude toward God. Neither of the first two ele-

ments could exist without this, but it is well for us to spell it out. There is new awareness of the holiness and justice of God, but there must also be a recognition of his amazing and abundant grace and mercy.

Repentance comes from a true view of God. If he should mark iniquities, none could stand; but there is forgiveness with him, that he may be feared (Ps. 130:3-4). Evangelical repentance, the inauguration and continuance of this life of godly fear, is always suffused with the promise and hope of forgiveness. That is why, for example, the repentance of the people of God in the days of Ezra was encouraged by the prospect, "there is still hope for Israel" (Ezra 10:2).

In the Gospels, Simon Peter's genuine repentance after his denial of Christ seems to be set in deliberate contrast with Judas' worldly sorrow and ultimate despair. It was produced by his remembering the word of the Lord, which in this case included the promise, "I have prayed for you, Simon, that your faith may not fail. And when you have turned back, strengthen your brothers" (Luke 22:32). The kindness of Christ led Peter to repentance (Rom. 2:4).

This was also the wise teaching of confessing Christians in the past:

> By it [repentance] a sinner, out of the sight and sense not only of the danger, but also of the filthiness and odious-ness of his sins, as contrary to the holy nature and righ-

teous law of God, *and upon the apprehension of his mercy in Christ to such as are penitent*, so grieves for and hates his sins, as to turn from them all unto God, purposing and endeavoring to walk with him in all the ways of his commandments. (*Westminster Confession of Faith*, XV, ii)

CHAPTER THREE

DAVID:
A CASE STUDY

We have established the fact that we need to repent and must repent constantly. How are we to do that? Here we may turn to Psalm 51, a psalm that was written by David to help us answer this question. Because he had discovered forgiveness himself, David writes to "teach transgressors [God's] ways" so that "sinners will turn back to [him]" (v. 13).

Arthur Weiser says that Psalm 51 is

not the fleeting mood of a depressed conscience, but the clear knowledge of a man who, shocked by that knowledge [of his sinfulness] has become conscious of his responsibility; it is a knowledge which excludes every kind of self-deception, however welcome it might be, and sees things as they really are. (*The Psalms, A Commentary* [Harrisburg, Penn.: SCM Press, 1962], pp. 403)

Psalm 51 was composed after David was confronted about his adultery with Bathsheba and his complicity in the murder of her husband Uriah. He had been brought to himself through the word of the court prophet Nathan (2 Sam. 11—12), and now he traces the pathway of repentance through which he discovered God's mercy. There are several important steps or stages along this pathway of repentance.

DISCOVERING THE TRUTH

David had discovered the truth about himself. His soul was like an onion, with layer upon layer of self-deception and pretense keeping him from recognizing his true spiritual condition. But this had been stripped away, and he now confesses his sin in a series of vivid word-pictures.

Verse 1. "Transgressions" (*pesha*) implies self-assertiveness. David's folly was to make himself the center of the universe, which is what sin always does. Sin marginalizes any rival, man (e.g., Uriah) or God. Having served well in the past as a faithful warrior and servant like David is no excuse for present sin.

Verse 2. "Iniquity" (*awon*) expresses a twistedness or

distortion that destroys everything. As a sinner, I have a fatal flaw. Made for God's glory, I have fallen short of it (Rom. 3:23). Instead of glorifying him in a God-centered life, I glorify myself and thus pervert what I am. Instead of enjoying God forever, in the end, if I do not turn to Christ, I will enjoy nothing forever.

Verses 2-3. "Sin" (*chattath*) denotes failure. David has missed the mark. Like the prodigal, he has squandered his destiny.

Verse 4. "Evil" (*ra*) is evil against God. He had done what was wrong in God's sight. Until now he had judged everything on the horizontal level: "Everyone does it; and anyway, I'm the king." Now God had opened his eyes to the shocking truth about himself. Evil deeds are the fruit of an evil heart. They are not an aberration from our true self but a revelation of it.

When we face up to the real nature of sin, we use honest words to describe ourselves: "transgressions . . . iniquity . . . sin . . . evil." We begin to use the first person singular, speaking of *my* transgressions, *my* iniquity, *my* sin, *my* evil. It is *my* fault. "I have sinned against heaven and against you. I am no longer worthy," said the prodigal (Luke 15:21). We no longer avoid the truth. It is *I* who lack "truth in the inner parts" (Ps. 51:6). Nor is this a new failure: "Surely I have been a sinner from birth, sinful from the time my mother conceived me," said David (v. 5). This last line is not an avoidance tactic. It means that at last I see that sin is woven into the very core of my being. I am congenitally, inescapably sinful. This is what I really am.

Only when I have seen this and cried out like that do I see my need for grace. And only those who have tasted the depths of their need can taste the sweetness of God's forgiveness. Only that self-discovery leads us to experience the cleansing pain of the live coal from the altar of God (Isa. 6:6-7). It burns and is painful, but it brings forgiveness.

THE EFFECTS OF SIN

We have a tendency to try to speed up repentance, because we feel we can cope with its pain only so long. It is a mark of grace in David's life that he sees that God's ways are slower, deeper, and wiser than ours.

What does sin do to us? Its effects are manifold.

1. *Sin produces guilt.* "I know my transgressions, and my sin is always before me" (v. 3). David's repentance began when his hard heart was pierced. Then the flood of guilt-feelings that flowed was uncontrollable. David could not stop it; he was profoundly guilty. That is why his prayer is not "Make me feel better" but "Have mercy on me!"

2. *Sin causes defilement.* Sin is multidimensional ("transgressions," "iniquity," "sin," "evil"), and its defilement pen-

etrates deeply. David's desire for a divine remedy underlines this. He feels as if his sins have been recorded on a clay tablet. So he pleads, "Blot out my transgressions" (v. 1). That is, break the tablet, destroy all the permanent records of my guilt. This is my only hope, for "if you, O LORD, kept a record of sins, O LORD, who could stand?" (Ps. 130:3). The guilt of sin is like an indelible dye staining his life and character. "Wash away all my iniquity," he pleads (v. 2). "Multiply washings" is what he actually says.

In my home country of Scotland it was unusual forty years ago for an ordinary family to possess a washing machine. As young boys we played soccer on dirt playing fields, not on grass, and our school matches frequently took place in the winter rain. My mother scrubbed the dirt out of my soccer gear with the help of a scrubbing board covered with rounded metal ridges. It was arduous work as she manually beat out the ingrained dirt. It was rough on her hands, not to mention the clothes!

That is the kind of picture David has in mind. We cannot get the dirt out by ourselves, as Jeremiah points out:

> *"Although you wash yourself with soda*
> *and use an abundance of soap,*
> *the stain of your guilt is still before me,"*
> *declares the Sovereign LORD.*

> —Jer. 2:22

God alone can scrub my heart clean. So David prays, "Cleanse me from my sin" (v. 2). Though the tears of a penitent heart wash the dirt from our vision and enable us to see the truth about ourselves, only God can cleanse our consciences from guilt.

3. *Sin leads to folly and self-deceit.* Sin makes us foolish, which is why I need to learn "wisdom in the inmost place" (v. 6). I deceive myself by my sin. In my folly I thought that God did not see me or detect my thoughts, or that he does not care about sin, or that sin does not have devastating consequences, or that it does not matter.

James's words, written much later, almost seem to be a commentary on David's experience: "Each one is tempted when, by his own evil desire [David, not God or Bathsheba, was responsible for his sin], he is dragged away and enticed. Then, after desire has conceived, it gives birth to sin [spiritual adultery in David's case was also physical adultery]; and sin, when it is full-grown [lust led to adultery, adultery led to murder], gives birth to death [Bathsheba gave birth, and the baby died]" (1:14-15). The next verse needs to be engraved upon our hearts: "Don't be deceived, my dear brothers" (v. 16).

When we share this sense of sinfulness and realize our powerlessness to deal with it, we learn to cry with David that

God will do something new: "Create in me a pure heart, O God" (v. 10).

The verb David uses here (*bara*) occurs first in the creation narrative in Genesis 1. God is always its subject. It describes a creative act that he alone can perform. David recognized this. Only God can change me; only God can make me pure; only God can make my heart willing.

4. *Sin places us in danger.* David prays, "Save me from bloodguilt" (v. 14), or better, "deadly guilt." He cannot bear the rigors of the divine analysis. "Hide your face from my sins," he cries (v. 9). Yet he fears even more that God might abandon him: "Do not cast me from your presence" (v. 11).

This is the greatest danger of all. God knows everything we may try to conceal. To him our hearts are always open books. No wonder, then, that David fears God will cast him into the outer darkness, which means out of his presence (v. 11). If that happens, the Aaronic blessing ("The Lord make his face shine upon you," Num. 6:25) will be only a memory. His sense of the absence of God will be permanent; the sound of "joy and gladness" (v. 8) will never be heard again. He has no defense.

> Against you, you only, have I sinned
>   and done what is evil in your sight,
> so that you are proved right when you speak
>   and justified when you judge. (v. 4)

Before God every mouth must plead guilty. No other plea will be allowed. We cannot appeal to the quality of our lives, our good deeds, or our spirituality. Nor can we appeal to our confused ideas of God's justice. "He'll be fair with me" is true, but the reality is terrifying.

A PLEA FOR MERCY

How, then, can I "hear joy and gladness" (v. 8) and experience "the joy of . . . salvation" (v. 12)? Only by throwing myself on the grace of God. Thus we cry, "Have mercy on me." We remind ourselves of God's "unfailing love" and "great compassion" (v. 1). We plead, "Blot out . . . wash away . . . cleanse me" (vv. 1-2).

The Hebrew word for "compassion" (v. 1) is related to the word for the womb. So David is asking God to remember that he is a creature, designed by God in eternity, nourished and preserved by him throughout life. The child whom Bathsheba bore may already have died when David wrote these words; so David would have been acutely aware of the love-loss that a mother feels for a child who had once lived within her womb. Was he appealing desperately to whatever in the heart of God is reflected in such love? Will God not hear the cry of a heart that is crushed and broken?

David is appealing to God's covenant-love (*chesedh*), the

love to which God has committed himself, even obligated himself in his covenant- promise to his people.

Dare we say: "O God, obligate yourself to love me with a love that will save me from my guilt"? David did, although he could not have known what he was ultimately asking for. We *do* know. David was asking God ultimately to cover his Son with our guilt, to withdraw from Jesus the sense of his Father's love, and to provide us with forgiveness and cover us with his Son's righteousness in order that we might sense the fullness of his love. He was asking for Calvary. In asking to experience God's "unfailing love" I am doing the same.

Repentance unfolds in a recognition of the danger of sin. It places us under the judgment of God (v. 4), in danger of being cast away from him (v. 11), and it involves an uncovering of the deep-seated intransigence of sin (v. 5), since it is rooted in our nature, from the very womb.

In light of this, true repentance inevitably involves "a broken spirit" (v. 17). That is different, observably different, from a highly emotional spirit. It is a spirit in which self-sufficiency and self-defense have been penetrated and broken down. Yet repentance also arises in the context of the hope of pardon. Appeal is made to the steadfast love of the Lord (v. 1); the cry of the penitent is directed to the One who is able to save and who does save (v. 14). The reality of such repentance is evidenced in a new concern for holiness. True repentance, because it is drawn out in the context of grace, also leads to and puts energy into worship: "O LORD, open my lips, and my mouth will declare your praise" (v. 15). Psalm 51 indicates that a view of God as holy and merciful, being a right view of him, is the only foundation for genuine evangelical repentance. His holiness grounds its necessity; his grace and mercy ground its possibility.

Herein, then, lies the importance of Luther's statement. Repentance does not merely begin the Christian life. According to Scripture, the Christian life is repentance from beginning to end! So long as the believer is *simul justus et peccator* (at the same time righteous and yet a sinner), it can be no other way.

CHAPTER FOUR

A MEDIEVAL THREAT

Little did Martin Luther realize that by nailing his theses to the Wittenberg Castle Church door, he simultaneously "nailed" the Gospel of Christ into the heart of the church. He was calling Christendom to repentance.

> Repentance which is occupied with thoughts of peace is hypocrisy. There must be a great earnestness about it and a deep hurt if the old man is to be put off. When lightning strikes a tree or a man, it does two things at once—it rends the tree and swiftly slays the man. But it also turns the face of the dead man and the broken branches of the tree itself toward heaven. (Bainton, *Here I Stand,* p. 48)

Luther's emphasis on the radical and lifelong character of repentance is the common testimony of the Reformers. John Calvin, Luther's younger French contemporary, taught that repentance is really the concrete expression of divine regeneration and renewal. In fact, Calvin *defines* regeneration as repentance (as the chapter title of his *Institutes of the Christian Religion* [Philadelphia: Westminster, 1960], III, iii, 1 makes plain). Even more, Calvin provides us with an in-depth exegesis of what repentance is, showing that it can never be separated from faith, though it should not be confused with it.

According to Calvin, repentance involves a threefold cord: "denial of ourselves, mortification of our flesh, and meditation on the heavenly life" (*Commentary on the Acts of the Apostles, 14-28* [Grand Rapids, Mich.: Eerdmans, 1966], p. 176).

This means that true repentance can never be reduced to a single act found only at the beginning of the Christian life. It arises in the context of our union with Jesus Christ; and since its goal is our restoration into the image of Christ, it involves the ongoing practical outworking of our union with Christ in his death and resurrection—what Calvin calls *mortification* and *vivification* (*Institutes*, III, iii, 3)—that is, being conformed to Christ crucified and risen.

It is not only my life as an individual that must be repentance-shaped, however. This must also be true of the whole church united to Christ by the Holy Spirit. Repentance is worked out both inwardly and outwardly in entire communities of believers. Thus says Calvin:

[Peter] teaches us that the government of the Church of Christ has been so divinely constituted from the beginning that the Cross has been the way to victory, death the way to life, and that this had been clearly testified. (*The Epistle of Paul the Apostle to the Hebrews, the Epistles of Peter* [Grand Rapids, Mich.: Eerdmans, 1963], p. 240)

MEDIEVALISM REVIVED

The Reformers' emphasis on repentance was set against the background of medieval theology. But rather than render their teaching irrelevant for us, this actually provides the key to its contemporary relevance. Once again we need to proclaim the full-orbed doctrine of repentance within an evangelical world that has begun to manifest symptoms of the same medieval sickness.

None of us is capable of an infallible analysis of the condition of the church in the West at the beginning of the third millennium. Nor should any of us despise the host of good things God has produced in his people. Thank God there are multitudes of congregations, some very large, some small, some well-known, some obscure, where there is a serious and joyful determination to give Jesus Christ his crowned rights in faithfulness to his Word, to live in his Spirit, to worship in his name, and to love his Father. But having said this, must we not also say that Christ has something against us (Rev. 2:4, 14, 20)?

There is a medieval darkness encroaching on evangelicalism. Yet sadly, many of its features are welcomed as though they are some fresh light or insight. Thus the possibility of a new "Babylonian or (more accurately, pagan) captivity of the church" looms nearer and larger than we may believe. Here is the evidence.

1. *Repentance is seen as an initial emotion, not as a vital part of a lifelong restoration of godliness.*

Seeing repentance as an isolated, completed act at the beginning of the Christian life is a principle underlying much of modern evangelicalism. We look back upon a single act, abstracted from its consequences, as determinative of salvation. In this subtle way, the modern "altar call" has become the evangelical equivalent of the sacrament of penance. For us, as for the medieval church, repentance has been divorced from genuine regeneration, and sanctification has been severed from justification.

Recently some evangelical Christians have been involved in what has come to be known as the "lordship salvation controversy," asking, "Can Christ be our Savior, yet not our Lord? Can we believe without being sanctified?" The controversy has deep and sophisticated theological and historical roots, deeper than some of its participants seem to have

THE GRACE OF REPENTANCE

realized. Yet it is a controversy that Luther settled with his first thesis. The idea that it is possible to receive justification without sanctification, to trust in a Savior who does not actually or presently save, to receive a new birth that does not actually give new life, or to have a faith that is not radically repentant despite uniting us to a crucified and risen Christ simply did not find a place in Reformation theology.

Paul spelled this out with perfect clarity, writing that "those who belong to Christ Jesus *have* [that is, have already] crucified the sinful nature with its passions and desires" (Gal. 5:24). To fail to live thus is, as Calvin vividly pointed out, to "rend [Christ] asunder by . . . mutilated faith" (*The Epistles of Paul the Apostle to the Romans and the Thessalonians* [Grand Rapids, Mich.: Eerdmans, 1960], p. 167).

At the dark perimeter of this aberrant theology lies the gospel of much televangelicalism. Tetzel-like, it peddles its wares on the small screen, implying, if not actually openly claiming, that the blessing of God can be purchased financially rather than being received only penitentially. Tetzel said:

> *As soon as the coin in the coffer rings*
> *The soul from purgatory springs.*

But there is a contemporary version found nowhere except in evangelicalism that goes:

42

As soon as the check in my pocket arrives
Comes increase in blessing—
*   that's no surprise.*

We need to cry, Enough! "When our Lord and Master, Jesus Christ, said 'repent,' he meant that the entire life of believers should be one of repentance."

2. *The practical rule of faith by which Christians live has increasingly been sought in a "Spirit-inspired" living voice within the church rather than in the Spirit's inscripturated voice in the Bible.*

In large sectors of evangelicalism, charismatic and non-charismatic alike, continuing "revelation" is enthusiastically welcomed. In a previous generation this came to clearest expression in those who expected to find guidance by "listening to the Spirit." The mainstream Reformers such as Luther and Calvin, and the great Puritans such as John Owen and the evangelists of the Great Awakening, were familiar with such "spirituality." Adding to, or sometimes bypassing, the voice of the Spirit in Scripture, the voice of the Spirit was supposed to be heard directly. Then, as now, some claimed to believe in the infallibility of the Bible but did not understand or rightly appreciate the Scripture's sufficiency.

Sadly, what was once little more than a mystical tendency has now become a flood. Those who hold to the Reformers' doctrine of the absolute sufficiency of Scripture, illumined by the work of the Spirit in the heart, are a decreasing breed. In academic theology, as well as at the grass roots of evangelicalism, the Reformers' position is becoming increasingly regarded as reactionary.

This equation—inscripturated word + living voice = divine revelation—lay at the heart of the medieval church's existence. It is one of the reasons the Roman Church—which is committed to two sources of revelation in any case—has managed to contain and then integrate the charismatic movement. Today, at the start of the third millennium, we are on the verge—and perhaps more than the verge—of being overwhelmed by a parallel phenomenon.

3. *God's presence was conveyed by an individual who claimed sacred powers and communicated them by physical means.*

As the Council of Trent (1545-1563) underlined, the medieval doctrine of orders (ordination) imprinted an indelible character on the priest ("On the Sacraments in General," Canon IX), who, through the words of the Mass (*hoc est corpus meum*, "this is my body"), could change bread and wine into the body and blood of Jesus. Though the "accidents" of bread and wine remained, the "substance" became the body and blood of the Lord. Thus, with his hands the priest could literally put Jesus into your mouth.

Today an uncanny parallel is visible wherever cable

television is available. It is no longer Jesus who is given by priestly hands; now it is the Spirit who is bestowed by physical means, apparently at will by the new evangelical priest. Slaying, healing, blowing, touching for blessing—these are the sacraments of the new millennium. How salutary to remember that the Reformers were told that they did not really have the Gospel because their church had no physical miracles!

What we ought to find alarming about contemporary evangelicalism is the extent to which we are similarly more impressed by performance than by piety. In the midst of the plethora of claims to the physical manifestations of the Spirit, knowing and being known by Christ in a life of sheer godliness has been discounted.

4. *Worship is increasingly becoming a spectator event of visual and sensory power, rather than a verbal event in which we engage in a deep soul dialogue with the Triune God.*

Contemporary evangelicalism tends to focus on what "happens" in a spectacle rather than on what is heard in worship. Aesthetics, be they artistic or musical, are given priority over bowing underneath the authority of what God says. More and more is *seen*; less and less is *heard*. There is a sensory feast but a hearing famine. This is purely medieval, not evangelical.

Preaching did not cut any ice in the Middle Ages. So the

people were given circuses—the medieval mystery plays. It is likewise today. Professionalism in presentation replaces power in the pulpit. Worship leadership is in danger of becoming a cheap substitute for genuine access to heaven, however faltering. Drama, not preaching, technological visuals, not an understanding of the Word, have become the *didache* of choice. The tragedy is that, whatever good intentions are pres-ent in this medievalism, its proponents do not seem to realize that the medieval plays were a confession of the impoverishment of the pulpit.

This is a spectrum, of course, not a single point. But most worship is to be found somewhere on that spectrum. There was a time when four simple words were enough to bring out goose bumps on the neck of our ancestors: "Let us worship God." Not so for twentieth- and twenty-first-century evangelicals. Now there must be color, movement, and audiovisual effects. God cannot be known, loved, praised, and trusted for his own sake.

We have lost sight of great things—the fact that Christ himself is the true sanctuary of the new-covenant people, that true beauty is holiness, that when the Lord is in his temple all are transfixed with a heart of silence before him. These are the glories of worship.

We have also more subtly lost sight of the transportability of new-covenant worship. By comparison with old-covenant worship, which depended on the temple, the new was simple *and therefore universalizable*. That was part of the vision that drove our evangelical forefathers. Much of our worship has become dependent on place, size, and, alas, even technology.

No church can afford smugly to point the finger of scorn and derision at evangelicals who have sold their heritage for a mess of modern pottage. In how many of our services is there such a sense of God's overwhelming presence that outsiders fall on their faces and cry out, "God is really among you!" (1 Cor. 14:25)?

We must offer our very best to God in corporate worship. But we do that only when we realize that true worship is not a spectator event, where we luxuriate in what others do. It is a *congregational* event, in which Christ mediates our prayers, conducts and leads our praise, and preaches his word to us. He alone is the God-ordained worship leader, the true minister in the sanctuary (Heb. 8:2). We dare not obscure this Christ-centered and congregational character, nor make worship dependent on anything other than approaching God in the Spirit through Christ with clean hands and a pure heart. The Father seeks such to worship him!

The tragedy of medieval worship was that God was no longer heard with penetrating clarity in the exposition of Scripture. And when the sense of the Spirit's presence was

no longer a reality, the order of the day became visual, col-
orful ritual rather than true liturgy, mystery (Latin!) rather
than plain speaking, color rather than clarity of doctrinal
understanding, drama (the medieval plays) rather than the
doctrine that would give them the knowledge of God. No
longer did the Word of God nourish souls and make them
morally and spiritually strong. A spiritual vacuum was created; collapse was inevitable.

For some time now there have been evidences in evangelicalism that we are on a slippery slope to neo-medieval-
ism. But sadly, it has been liberal observers and critics rather
than evangelical leaders who have been first to point out the
decline.

In the summer of 1978 I had the memorable privilege
of speaking at a conference along with the great Welsh
preacher Dr. D. Martyn Lloyd-Jones. One of his addresses
on that occasion was entitled "Extraordinary Phenomena in
Revivals of Religion." It was an extraordinary phenomenon
in itself. Ninety minutes in length, it seemed like fifteen. I
was gripped and fascinated to hear of incidents—largely in
Wales—that eyewitnesses had described to him.

Lloyd-Jones mentioned a relatively recent, well-known
Welsh evangelist whose "trademark" was the fact that he
played an instrument during the evangelistic meetings he
conducted. On one occasion his father urged him to put it

aside, noting that his generation of ministers had not needed such embellishments. "No, Dad," came the reply. "But *you had the Holy Spirit*."

Thus we condemn ourselves.

The tragedy here is that in our worship we are in danger of producing a generation of professing Christians who remain spiritual infants, feeding them emotionally with what produces satisfaction for a brief moment but never truly builds them up in Christ.

I once heard Dr. James Montgomery Boice express this principle as he introduced congregational prayer for Sunday school teachers at Tenth Presbyterian Church in Philadelphia. He noted that from the beginning the children are taught small portions of Scripture on which they build until, for example, they are eventually able to recite such chapters of the Bible as Romans 8. Hymns (yes, hymns!) are sung and learned because of their power to teach doctrine (yes, doctrine!).

Why this stark contrast with, if not opposition to, the trends of the time? Here, as I recall, is what Dr. Boice gave as the rationale: "We are living in a time when adults, including Christians, want to behave like children. Here, in our Sunday school, we are training our children to grow up to be Christian adults."

How smug we have become—we who know too much

about child psychology to care about the Catechism or perhaps even Scripture itself! Alas, some of our leaders do not know as much Christian doctrine as a child in Calvin's Geneva, have only half the grasp of man's chief end that a girl in the remote fastnesses of seventeenth-century Scotland might have had, and seem to know far less about how to overcome sin than a teenager in John Owen's Oxford.

5. *Ministry growth is measured by crowds and cathedrals ("mega-churches") rather than by the preaching of the Cross and the quality of Christians' lives.*

It was the medieval church leaders—bishops and archbishops, cardinals and popes—who built cathedrals, ostensibly for God's glory—*soli Deo gloria*. But it was to the neglect of gospel proclamation, the life of the body of Christ as a whole, the needs of the poor, and the evangelism of the world. The "mega-church" is not a modern but a medieval phenomenon.

Ideal congregational size and ecclesiastical architecture are questions on which Scripture does not specifically pronounce, and that is not really the central concern. Rather, the central issue is the almost endemic addiction of contemporary evangelicalism to size and numbers as an index of the success of "ministry."

Here, too, there is something reminiscent of the Middle Ages. It was, after all, the building of a sanctuary for a "mega-church" (St. Peter's in Rome) that provoked the Reformation! How much indulgence selling and buying goes on in contemporary church life? How much of the medieval desire for a *kathedra* (throne) for the leader or leaders comes to expression in the huge, staggering buildings we erect "for the glory of God"?

This is not a plea for a new evangelical iconoclasm; smaller is not necessarily better or more beautiful. Nevertheless, it is a plea to raise questions about reality, depth, and integrity in contemporary church life and in the Christian ministry. Inevitably, the lust for "bigger" makes us materially and financially vulnerable. But worse, it makes us spiritually vulnerable. For it is hard to say to those on whom we have come to depend financially, "When our Lord and Master, Jesus Christ, said 'repent,' he meant that the entire life of believers should be one of repentance."

What are we to do with Luther's spine-chilling Thesis 93 in light of our watered-down gospel and debased church practices?

> Hail, hail to all those prophets who say to Christ's people,
> "The cross, the cross," where there is no cross.

Or Thesis 94? Can we proclaim this with a clear conscience?

THE GRACE OF REPENTANCE

Christians should be exhorted to be zealous to follow Christ, their Head, through penalties, deaths, and hells.

Or Thesis 95?

And let them thus be more confident of entering heaven through many tribulations rather than through a false assurance of peace.

When we look at today's evangelical churches, we may well wish that Luther's Theses had been left in the Latin in which he first penned them and thus kept within their original arena of academic dispute! Yet only when these notes ring out in our churches—only when we heed the Scriptures—can we be sure that we are building with gold, silver, and costly stones and not with wood, hay, and stubble. Only what we build in God's way will last for eternity. Everything else will be consumed by fire (1 Cor. 3:12-15).

CHAPTER FIVE

THE WAY BACK

If repentance is the lifelong process of the restoration of sinners, as we have seen, it must be an inescapable, ongoing, and permanent necessity. But how is repentance like this to be produced?

Here it is important for us not to write our agenda merely in terms of what is wrong with evangelicalism today. That exercise may be necessary, but it is only partial. What gives repentance power is not the *guilt* evoked by the Law alone (Rom. 7:7), but the *grace* proclaimed to us only in the Gospel of our Lord Jesus Christ. It is the kindness of God that leads to repentance (Rom. 2:4). It is only because there is forgiveness with God that we live lives of penitential fear (Ps. 130:4).

Wherever we see repentance in the Scriptures, this is the pattern. The revelation of divine holiness in the Law and commandments of God creates the guilt-burden. But then grace enables the guilt-burdened and heartbroken to repent. Repentance is possible because of the great promise of forgiveness. Knowing this, we can cry through our tears: "Have mercy . . . according to your unfailing love . . . according to your great compassion blot out my transgressions. . . . Cleanse me . . . wash me . . . Let me hear joy and gladness. . . . Hide your face from my sins and blot out all my iniquity. . . . Create in me a pure heart . . . renew a steadfast spirit within me. . . . Restore to me the joy of your salvation" (Ps. 51:1-12).

This happens only when we hear the cry, "The cross! The cross!" Sadly, just here evangelicalism has sometimes become like a latter-day Jonah, seeking prestige in the world rather than honor before God. It seeks to preserve its own *kudos* among its own kind. It sings about, but does not find, the cross "wondrous." It wears but does not bear the cross.

Only when we are humbled under the mighty hand of God can there be exaltation. We need first to see, Jonah-like, how far down we have sunk, to see our need of grace and the cross, and thus to find forgiveness and restoration. Like Jonah, there are two things from which we contemporary evangelicals flee.

First, *the word of the Lord that comes to us with great clarity* (Jonah 1:2). Now, we believe in the perspicuity of Scripture. Our problem, like Jonah's, does not lie in the parts of Scripture we find difficult to understand. Like him, we turn away from the word of the Lord that we *do* understand. We do not read it, we do not love it, we have become almost incapable of meditating upon it; we are careless, if not actually callous about submitting to it.

Second, *we often turn from the presence of God* (Jonah 1:3, 10). We cannot just sit still or silent before him. Prayer has become the hardest thing in the world for us to do. Poor Jonah! Poor evangelicalism!

Yet there is a way back. There is the sign of Jonah—the cross. And God has his ways of preparing winds to pursue us, great fish to swallow us, dark bellies that, as Calvin says, become hospitals to heal us of our deathly sickness. Will we need distress as a community to make us call on the Lord and turn back to his presence and his Word?

Liberal Old Testament scholars have frequently suggested that the prayer of Jonah 2 is simply a smart piece of authorial creativity because it is virtually a weaving together of quotations from the Psalms. (Have they never attended a church prayer meeting?) But that is precisely the point. The man could not get enough of Scripture. Like all who deeply repent, he wanted to devour it, turn it into prayer, bathe in it, and feed upon it; and he longed to put into practice everything it commanded. What he had vowed, he would make good (Jonah 2:9).

Jonah sought the presence of God and the worship of God. Banished in exile, he wanted his captivity to end. He wanted to be in the temple—where the portrayal of forgiveness could be found, where the praise of God could be heard, where the people of God could be met, where he could reaffirm his first vows of commitment to his Lord.

When Jonah repented, his heart was moved with compassion for the lost who "cling to worthless idols [and] forfeit the grace that could be theirs" (Jonah 2:8). But that happened only when he realized the grip the idols of his own heart had on him, and how tightly he had gripped them. Only then did it dawn on him with fresh power that "Salvation comes from the Lord" (Jonah 2:9). When that dawn comes, true evangelical repentance becomes the sweetest pain in the whole world.

Would we had a baptism of it!

CHAPTER SIX

WHAT SHALL WE DO?

Evangelicalism is a noble tradition. Shall we not learn from it? Our forefathers determined to live in the presence of God. They gathered to seek his presence and listen to his voice in the exposition and application of Scripture. They built communities of Christ with precious stones hewn at great cost from deep quarries. They eschewed wood and hay and stubble. They knew they would stand before the judgment seat of Christ to receive what was due them for the things they had done in the body (2 Cor. 5:10). They lived, labored, prayed, and built for eternity. So must we.

They asked for divine blessing, and they were heard. Alas, we have not because we have not asked; and even when we do ask, it is too often only to fulfill our sinful lusts (James 4:2-3). We must know that the Kingdom has come in Jesus Christ. We must repent and believe the Gospel.

THE GRACE OF REPENTANCE

We must begin the road to recovery by confessing our guilt. Unlike our forefathers we do this with great infrequency. Evangelicalism has tended to present an appearance of moral one-upmanship rather than the tear-stained face of repentance. We are so unskilled in confession that we must look around desperately to ask, Who can bear the weight of being the mouthpiece of confession for sins such as ours? We are such neophytes in this matter. We stumble at repentance, and we do not know where to turn for help.

Yet here again our forefathers can come to our aid.

The Confession and Catechisms drawn up by the Westminster Assembly between 1643 and 1648 are well known. Less well known is the fact that four years later the ministers of the Church of Scotland, having embraced these grand doctrinal statements, recognized their need not only to confess the doctrines of the faith but also the sins of their own lives as an essential starting point for ongoing repentance.

Those were critical days, but by no means wholly barren spiritually. There were many evidences of God's preserving goodness and numerous ministries of outstanding godliness, grace, power, and fruitfulness. Those were days when Puritan giants could be met in the streets of London, Oxford, and many other places. It was surely evidence of even greater stirrings of God when these Christian leaders corporately confessed their faults.

What follows is part of their confession of their sins *as Christian leaders*. May God use it to help us in self-examination.

Guidance in Confession

Ignorance of God, want [lack] of nearness with him, and taking up little of God in reading, meditating and speaking of him. Exceeding great selfishness in all that we do; acting from ourselves, for ourselves and to ourselves.

Not caring how faithful and negligent others were, so being it might contribute a testimony to our faithfulness and diligence, but being rather content, if not rejoicing, at their faults.

Least delight in those things wherein lieth our nearest communion with God; great inconstancy in our walk with God, and neglect of acknowledging him in all our ways. In going about duties, least careful about those things which are most remote from the eyes of men. Seldom in secret prayer with God, except to fit for public performance; and even that much neglected, or gone about very superficially.

Glad to find excuses for the neglect of our duties. Neglecting the reading of Scripture in secret, for edifying ourselves as Christians. . . . Not given to reflect upon our own ways, nor allowing conviction to have a thorough work upon us; deceiving ourselves by resting upon absence from and abhorrence of evils from the light of a natural conscience, and looking upon the same as an evidence of a real change of state and nature.

Not esteeming the cross of Christ and sufferings for his name honorable, but rather shifting sufferings from self-love.

Not laying to heart the sad and heavy sufferings of the people of God abroad, and the not-thriving of the kingdom of Jesus Christ and the power of godliness among them.

Refined hypocrisy; desiring to appear what, indeed, we are not. Studying more to learn the language of God's people than their exercise. Artificial confessing of sin, without repentance; professing to declare iniquity, and not resolving to be sorry for sin. Confession in secret much slighted, even of those things whereof we are convicted.

Readier to search out and censure faults in others than to see or deal with them in ourselves. Accounting of our estate and way according to the estimate that others have of us.

Estimation of men, as they agree or disagree from us.

Fruitless conversing ordinarily with others, for the worse rather than for the better. Foolish jesting away of time with . . . useless discourse.

Slighting of fellowship with those by whom we might profit, desiring more to converse with those that might better us by their talents than with such as might edify us by their graces.

Not studying opportunities of doing good to others. Shifting of prayer and other duties when called thereto . . . loving our pleasures more than God.

Not praying for men of a contrary judgment, but using reservedness and distance from them; being more ready to speak *of* them than to them, or to God *for* them.

Not preaching Christ in the simplicity of the gospel, nor ourselves the people's servants, for Christ's sake. Preaching of Christ, not that the people may know him, but that they may think we know much of him. . . . Not preaching with bowels of compassion to them that are in hazard to perish.

Bitterness, instead of zeal, in speaking against malignants, sectarians and other scandalous persons. . . . Too much eying our own credit and applause; and being pleased with it when we get it, and unsatisfied when it is wanting. . . . Not making all the counsel of God known to his people. (In Horatius Bonar, *Words to Winners of Souls* [Philadelphia: Presbyterian and Reformed, 1995], pp. 25-34)

There is surely much more we need to confess. Ought we not to make a beginning now? Does it not remain true that unless we repent, our churches will all likewise perish?

FOR FURTHER READING

Armstrong, John H., editor. *The Coming Evangelical Crisis: Current Challenges to the Authority of Scripture and the Gospel.* Chicago: Moody Press, 1996.

——. *The Compromised Church: The Present Evangelical Crisis.* Wheaton, Ill.: Crossway Books, 1998.

Boice, James Montgomery and Sasse, Benjamin E., editors. *Here We Stand: A Call from Confessing Evangelicals.* Grand Rapids, Mich.: Baker, 1996.

Calvin, John. *The Institutes of the Christian Religion,* trans. F. L. Battles; ed. John T. McNeill. Philadelphia: Westminster Press, 1960.

Horton, Michael Scott, editor. *Power Religion: The Selling Out of the Evangelical Church?* Chicago: Moody Press, 1992.

Kistler, Don, editor. *Sola Scriptura: The Protestant Position on the Bible.* Morgan, Penn.: Soli Deo Gloria Publications, 1995.

MacArthur, John F. *Ashamed of the Gospel: When the Church Becomes Like the World.* Wheaton, Ill.: Crossway Books, 1993.

Wells, David F. *No Place for Truth: Or Whatever Happened to Evangelical Theology?* Grand Rapids, Mich.: Wm. B. Eerdmans, 1993.

——. *The Bleeding of the Evangelical Church.* Edinburgh: Banner of Truth Trust, 1995.

ALLIANCE®

OF CONFESSING EVANGELICALS

The Alliance of Confessing Evangelicals is a coalition of Christian leaders from various denominations (Baptist, Presbyterian, Reformed, Congregational, Anglican, and Lutheran) committed to promoting a modern reformation of North America's church in doctrine, worship, and life, according to Scripture. We seek to call the twenty-first century church to a modern reformation through broadcasting, events, publishing, and distribution of reformed resources.

The work centers on broadcasting—*The Bible Study Hour* with James Boice, *Every Last Word* featuring Philip Ryken, *God's Living Word* with Bible teacher Richard Phillips, and *Dr. Barnhouse & the Bible* with Donald Barnhouse. These broadcasts air daily and weekly throughout North America as well as online and via satellite.

Our events include the Philadelphia Conference on Reformed Theology, the oldest, continuing, national, reformed conference in North America; many regional events including theology and exposition conferences and pastors' events, including Reformation Societies who continue to join the hearts and minds of church leaders in pursuit of reformation in the church.

reformation21 is our online magazine—a free "go-to" theological resource. We also publish *God's Word Today* online daily devotional; *MatthewHenry*.org, a source on biblical prayer; Alliance Books from a list of diverse authors; and more.

The Alliance further seeks to encourage reformation in the church by offering a wide variety of CD and MP3 resources featuring Alliance broadcast speakers and many other nationally recognized pastors and theologians.